To John

You're never alone with schizophrenia

PARABLES OF A SCHIZOPHRENIC POET

PARABLES OF A SCHIZOPHRENIC POET: POEMS, PROSE AND REFLECTIONS TO ENLIGHTEN THOSE WITH TIRED MINDS

Other works by Alan Swift

Psychotic Symptoms

Homage

(Available from lulu.com)

First Printing: 2014

ISBN: 978-1-291-91695-9

Alan.swift348@btinternet.com
swozza@hotmail.co.uk

DEDICATION

I dedicate this work to my late Mother and Father, Mary Parr and Bernard Swift and to the Muse who has recently graced me with Her company once more;

Thank You!

ACKNOWLEDGEMENTS

I would like to thank my fiancée Joan Cummings for her love, patience and continued support; Peter Fleming for his encouragement and friendship; Terry Caffrey and the poetry circle at the Citadel in St. Helens and you dear reader for perusing this tome!

PREFACE

The Muse, my lover, has returned with a vengeance! I've recently started composing new material after the success of my two previous works, Psychotic Symptoms and Homage, which were a revamping of some of my older works from a dark era nearly 20 years ago.

Although I still have my dark days and find mornings hard to adjust to, I am generally of a more jovial disposition than in my earlier days of coping with the reality, or unreality, of a diagnosis of schizophrenia in the year of 1987.
How do I cope you may ask and if you suffer or know someone who has a label this book may help. It is a testimony to the reality that it is possible to live a happy life despite the circumstances and I am proof of that. What I've found helpful, to varying degrees is a sense of purpose, meditation, biofeedback techniques, cognitive behavioural therapy, New Age and Buddhist philosophies, voluntary work, a loving partner, friendship, telling jokes and tall tales, eating out and drinking in coffee bars, going to the cinema and watching comedies and inspirational videos, reading, walking and playing the Native American Flute (check out Mr Swozza on YouTube!).

So courage my friend, and with age comes wisdom and contentment
,
Happy Reading

Alan Swift

14 Jun. 14

TABLE OF CONTENTS

dedication 7

acknowledgements 8

preface 9

act i: scene iv 14

the game of life 15

what do i want out of life? 16

i reacted to that! 17

reflections 18

sanctuary.. 19

competition... 20

tribute to alan watts 21

i am resting 22

idea... 23

the meaning of life 24

hugs, not drugs (or i need a kiss) 25

sometimes... 26

the quest 27

illusions of nature 28

life is a dream.. 29

subliminal seduction 30

why waste your time with this poem when you could be
getting laid 32

the trench.. 33

Alan Swift

a digression of words 34

h2o 35

the day of wrath........... 36

subliminal seduction revisited 38

rambling on my mind........... 39

journey........... 40

surrender or die 41

verbal meanderings 42

amusing musings of muse........... 44

poco in roman times 46

poetry or pleasure........... 47

thoughts in my head 48

i can see it in the future 50

teach me to listen 51

reflections 52

two faced 53

morning time colours........... 54

space 55

for all the times i forgot 56

power thinking with brother mandus........... 58

battlefield of the mind........... 60

life without reason........... 62

it's a beautiful day for dreaming........... 63

i need to talk to myself 64

blood on your plate... 66

purpose 67

why do poets bleed... 68

illusions 69

song of silence.. 70

within 70

words are but words... 71

alayana yakatana!.. 72

finale 73

Alan Swift

ACT I: SCENE IV

Here I go again,
Performing this role I call 'Me!'
Absorbed in this play called 'Life!'

At times I forget that it is a play,
But that is okay,
Tomorrow,
When it's over,
I'll remember,
It was just a story.

For now I play the scenes,
I recite my lines,
Like I've done so many times before,
Forgetting it's just a play,
And so I go in search,
In search of fulfilment,
In search of enlightenment,
I even go in search of myself;
(As if I could lose myself!)
Playing this role called 'Me!'
In this play called 'Life!'

THE GAME OF LIFE

You agreed to play before the banker dealt your hand. He gave you five cards and you looked at them with anticipation. You did not choose them, nor did the banker, he merely dealt them; fate provided. It does not matter. The cards you received are symbolic of the beginning of your journey, your journey through life.

Look at your cards. Maybe a good hand, maybe a bad hand, but what counts is how you play it. It's up to you. You could blame fate or the banker for a bad deal, but is there a bad deal. And remember, it's only a game and there'll be another round. Keep your cool and play your best and enjoy the game.

You may in disgust throw in your hand and complain of your misfortune. The choice is yours, there's nobody else to blame. They're your cards and yours alone. The other players will play their cards too, they may even forget it's just a game; play on regardless. It does not concern you.

Maybe their hands are better than yours, maybe they seem more skilful. Maybe they laugh, maybe they curse, do not let that bother you, it's just a game although you can treat it seriously if it helps you play better! And remember, if it all seems too much, there'll be another round and there'll always be another day and the more you play the greater will be your skill as it is in life.

WHAT DO I WANT OUT OF LIFE?

What do I want out of life? The mere fact of wanting something, an object or an experience, means I am not content in the present moment. And yet to want to avoid the experience of not feeling content is in itself a trap. Catch 22!

I am grateful for my feelings. Unfortunately they hold me back sometimes and I find it a struggle to do the things I need to do that I don't feel like doing. This has become worse with time and I now realise I need to do something about it. I have read a book about mini habits and I realise I can do certain tasks if I make them small enough and keep at them. The fear in my mind, the thoughts in my head, are that I'll not put this into practise and I'll slowly forget about it.

I need to clear my garden, a task I keep putting off. Equally off-putting is the thought of dusting the house and getting rid of some of my possessions that are cluttering my house. I'd like to exercise more and write a best seller.

It's all about mini habits so I could do five minutes gardening a day and five minutes dusting. Nay I could even do dusting one day and gardening the next and I dare say that I can manage to do two press ups a day to start and I've already started writing!

I REACTED TO THAT!

I reacted to that with fear!
I reacted to that with anger!
I reacted to that with resentment!
And thus I surrendered my control
Surrendered to external events
Surrendered to a power beyond me
To a power which does not exist,
Except in my imagination.

When the suitor's love is in gaol,
The gaol is the thief.
When I write lines with reason,
Where is there relief?

To think stifles my creativity,
And yet without focus or discipline,
My writing is vapid, fluffy and with little merit.

Ideas will come if you allow them,
Ideas will come if you acknowledge them,
Ideas will come if you appreciate them,
If you are still and listen,
Ideas will come,
So write them down
Before they disappear!

REFLECTIONS

Life at times seems strange. Just when I'm beginning to think I understand all things something unusual occurs. Take time for example. When time goes slow the day seems grim and full of woe. Yet when life is fun all is gone and done before I've even had time to blink. It seems a strange arrangement in which bad is made to endure whilst the good seems to fail and fade. How much easier it is to be upset by the bad and to forget the good. How much easier it is to form bad habits and lose good ones. Intentions are hard to keep and many people weep without our realising it. Yet the day will come to all when the tears will flow.

You may call me an optimist, deluded or simply insane, when I tell you despite the above, I believe that God is Love and all will be okay. I can't say why any more than I can explain life. I'm only human and despite all the strife my reason is sadly stunted. Even old Albert, Plato and Socrates were lost for words so all of my offerings are like hollowed out gourds, useless and tepid inspirations!

But there comes a time when the pressure builds up and the words must flow. In all profanity the king seeks solace and silence whilst the knave and the scoundrel increase their violence without sufficient reflection. Silence is good in a world of noise. Silence is necessary after words issue forth. Truth needs to be digested to be of any use; too much noise is a form of abuse that often becomes intolerable. There comes a time when you can tell humanity to keep its toys and trinkets, which dazzle the eyes with their glitter. Sometimes it is necessary to raise another litter of pups, and then nothing else matters.

SANCTUARY

Sanctuary I seek,
Here in your arms,
Just for today.

Inside and out,
Sanctuary is there,
In each time,
In each season,
Summer and winter,
Spring and fall
Sanctuary,
Ever changing.

A drop in the ocean,
A thought in God's mind,
Creator and created,
Interlinked and entwined,
Within and without,
There is peace to be found,
Here in sanctuary.

Hot or cold,
Young or old,
Happy or sad,
Good or bad,
All seek sanctuary,
And this is good,
This is sanctuary.

COMPETITION

No matter how far up you go there will always be someone ahead of you. There will always be desire as long as you live. Without it you would be dead; was Shakymuni a zombie?

Did Jesus ever catch a cold or get the runs or play with himself? And if not, why not?

SIN: Sex Is Normal
SIN: Someone Is Naked
SIN: Somewhat Inspired Notions
SIN: Society's Industrial Nations
SIN: Schizophrenia Is Normal

But don't be afraid, that is what the hidden powers want of you, for fear keeps you servant and yet we have created all this. Sure we've forgotten and it would seem blasphemy to say so but one day we'll all wake up.

Maybe your thoughts revolve creating paranoia. Maybe they judge reality falsely fabricating a hostile world, or maybe a happy world, or a neutral world. It all depends on how we feel. For thoughts and feelings create the experience.

TRIBUTE TO ALAN WATTS

I find myself thinking
As I write these words
That I am now reading,
Where am I?
And what am I?

Memory creates my perception,
Is it all a chaotic dream?
A strange somnambulistic scene?

Will I ever wake up?
Have I ever been born?
Have I simply dreamt
The last fifty years of my life?
Simply dreamt of this vast cosmos?

Am I really God?
Simply dreaming?

I AM RESTING

I am resting,
Awake, content and happy.
Basically,
My life is a breeze,
And I have no worries,
No concerns,
What is,
Is,
And so it shall be!
Who am I?
To argue with life?
To argue with death?
It's just a journey,
No,
It just is!
And so it shall be,
Now and forever,
Throughout eternity
Where time has no meaning,
And clocks are dismantled,
Thrown on the scrapheap,
Where the cuckoos are calling,
Amongst the deafening silence,
Amidst the ceaseless bustle,
Of divine repose,
Where God is my lover,
The Goddess my spouse,
And I like the Creator,
Am fulfilled.

IDEA

I offer this idea,
Take it my child,
It may serve you well,
Like the glass,
Which holds the liquid,
That quenches your thirst.

And this my child,
This is the idea,
An idea so profound,
So mind blowing,
That for centuries,
This has been denied,
For centuries,
This has been suppressed.

You are asleep,
Yes my child,
You are asleep,
This is a dream,
A fabrication of your mind,
And you cannot remember,
Who your Father is,
Sweet innocent Child of the Father!

THE MEANING OF LIFE

The meaning of life is not to be found in words lofty or deep. No, my son, it is to be found elsewhere! There comes a time in life when one realises that all previous quests and adventures were indeed futile. It comes as a shock to realise all of one's endeavours were to no avail and that one has wasted a lifetime searching for dreams in a land of mirages.

How quickly one comes to this conclusion will vary depending on circumstance and temperament, but come it will. Many false faiths and many false leads will be taken by those who begin the search, but that must not deter the aspirant for the journey of a thousand miles must begin with a single step.

Indeed it is possible to take the journey several times and still remain at home with the idea of salvation which merely whets the saliva of insanity as the beards of the elders merely whiten and lengthen as time marches on.

My words may be deep but the relations I keep more truly speak of my nature. Words lofty and profound are merely a sound in the void to the uninitiated. It is like talking to the wind when realisation has sinned against its conscience. No matter how deep I can but weep for words are inadequate. So the conclusion is clear that one should lay off the beer and earn oneself a living if one can!

HUGS, NOT DRUGS (OR I NEED A KISS)

We are alone and that is our fate;
Longing for connection,
We reach for each other
Puckering of lips
And closing our eyes,
We wish to merge,
To merge with each other.

Memories of heaven leave me restless,
And now I long for you,
For in heaven we were spirits,
And now we can embrace,
We can touch and caress;
Oh, the beauty of physical form,
Far beyond any ethereal dream;
This is bliss!
The joy of a kiss!

SOMETIMES

Sometimes I wonder why things work out the way things do! There are so many things which appear to be of no use to anyone. The world seems in a sorry state and it often seems, to me at least, to be going worse as time goes on. Am I getting old and cynical? Perhaps even clinical?

Sometimes the world seems pleasant and days and nights are charming. And yet at other times the world can be alarming! The media blows things out of proportion and gets paid for its service. Who is to say who is right? God alone is the judge to whom we must all go. All will die and only this I know. Perhaps it will all turn out okay, yet who am I to say?

Sometimes it is easy and sometimes it is hard. There is always someone worse off than us and there is always someone to be envious of. Justice is hard to come by these days. Technology makes things easier and brings new perils in its wake. Mass unemployment and aggression on humanity take their toll. Drug addicts and dropouts abound for all to see. Society is collapsing in a void of promiscuity.

Sometimes I preach and sometimes I pray. Sometimes I feel sad and sometimes grey. Yet life goes on and all is well; sometimes in heaven, other times in hell. The answer is clear for all to see. Sometimes I see it and sometimes I don't. It varies and changes and sometimes it won't.

Sometimes there's laughter and sometimes there's pain. Sometimes life seems jolly like a witty refrain but then there's rain, but only sometimes I'm glad to say. So the moral of this story is to take life as it comes, sometimes!

THE QUEST

You're secretly searching for God in that next coffee;
You're secretly searching for Him in that next pint;
You're secretly searching for Her in that next conquest.

You've lost all knowledge of God's presence,
You don't know where to find Her,
So, desperately,
Frantically,
You search and scour,
You look everywhere,
In sausages and soup,
From Sunday services to sex,
Not realising the Godhead within.

You will only find what you seek when you stop searching,
When you remember,
When you wake from your soulless slumber,
And then remember who you really are.

No longer a victim of life,
When you wake from the illusion,
Of powerlessness and victimhood,
And remember you are a child of God.

ILLUSIONS OF NATURE

The truth for all to see is that when possessions take possession of one's soul that it is clear that one has missed one's goal in life. What started out well-meaning is gleaning the maggots of today from the dung heaps of tomorrow, which can only lead to the learned response called frustration.

It is clear that one must work for the truth and to jerk one's knee in an unfashionable manner when one turns the spanner of circumstance before the sun goes down on today's opportunity. For an apology profound cannot be found to remedy a hopeless situation.

"Where is the answer?" is the question on the lips of the babe and the bearded professor, on that of the politician and priest, the born and deceased and all in-between. Yet who would have heard that the answer, absurd indeed, is not worth listening to. For if that were so, the answer of "No!" would be taken less seriously. In truth it does not matter.

LIFE IS A DREAM

Life is a dream in slow motion,
Films try to capture our dreams
Before they die,
And that is why they appeal to us.

A kiss in the movies is steamy,
A kiss in your fantasies and dreams is otherworldly,
But in reality a kiss is just a kiss.

Life is a dream in slow motion,
Films are dreams at full speed.

When the mind is sleeping
Life is unreal,
And yet who is dreaming?
And who is awake?

SUBLIMINAL SEDUCTION

You,
Like me,
Know good work
When you see it.

You,
Like me,
Want to,
Hear it,
Touch it,
Taste it,
Smell it,
Feel it.

You,
Like me,
Want to be,
Seduced,
Beguiled,
Led on,
Teased and captivated.

You,
Like me,
Are,
Romantic,
Wise,
And intelligent.

You,
Like me,

Love life,
Love fun,
Laughter,
And adventure.

You,
Like me,
Feel safe,
And secure.

You,
Like me,
Love trying new things,
Making new friends,
And pushing the boundaries.

You,
Like me,
Want to give it a go,
Right now,
And may I just say,
You,
Blow me away!

WHY WASTE YOUR TIME WITH THIS POEM WHEN YOU COULD BE GETTING LAID

Why am I writing when I could be having sex?
Why am I wondering will you spend all evening on your DS
when we could be having sex?

It's not that we don't fancy each other,
It's not that we're getting older,
Maybe we've got too comfortable?
Maybe we've got used to each other?
Maybe we've become too familiar to passionately copulate?
Too close to shag with abandon,
Unlike our earlier days.

Is this humanity's curse?
To watch the telly and to go to the gym,
To eat out in style,
And yet forget to fornicate?

Are we really too busy to bonk?
Why am I writing this?
Why are you still reading this?
When we could be having sex?

THE TRENCH

Death, like a demon, goes stalking,
Terror of the day,
Guardian of the night,
Alone I stand,
Surrounded by my comrades,
Wounded and dying.

Rain,
Cold,
Falls upon my mortal frame,
Blood, sweat, tears, faeces and mucus mingle,
In rivers of despair,
Etching themselves in the faces of fellow soldiers,
Cigarettes are distributed to calm the hysterical,
As the mustard gas cloud chokes,
Where mud is my name,
And life is a game,
I no longer wish to play.

Tired and hallucinating I slip into a fitful sleep,
My lover comes to me,
Mocking and menacing,
Even here I cannot escape,
For her form becomes a skeleton,
As I embrace her.

Just then a shell detonates,
Returning me to this nightmare,
I wish I was dead,
Yet maybe I am and this is Hell?

A DIGRESSION OF WORDS

Today I do not understand the reason for my misunderstanding in the field of the progress of technology. I can see the reason for aggression in the case of frustration but that does not justify it. How can I be realistic when I am an illusion? I cannot underestimate the reason for my unreasonableness or my infidelity to the cause, to which I ascribed so many eons ago. Today I act the toad as I walk down the road of society and justice whilst people starve and people cry; people are born and people die; but what is that to me if my stomach is full? It may sound cruel and I am the fool to say such things when infinity sings songs of wonder and woe into my ears for others to hear as the empire around us collapses. So what can I say but show me the day when God will appear to a mortal?

The truth is for all to see if you would agree with me it would be, oh so much easier. How do I know? All I can show is the march of technology is profound like the undertakers sound of disturbance. The trust of the people is what I need, the politician may plead as the soldier bleeds from wounds beyond redemption. How can I say that it's okay when people all around us are dying? May the truth be known as compost is thrown onto the weeds and the vines of resentment?

There is much to say but that is okay as long as you search for the answer. Alas it isn't that easy.

H2O

On that red planet called Mars,
Humans are looking for life,
Humans are looking for water,
But it's not there.

On that red planet called Mars,
There are no waterfalls,
And there are no little green men,
They are there no longer.

Yet eons before mankind came here,
Little green men on Mars did abide,
And drank deep from the streams,
Streams of cold water.

Yet one fateful day a comet from afar,
Hit that red planet, aha,
And left it bereft of water.

So the little green men sojourned to Earth,
In their spaceships so round
In search of water.

Yet the atmosphere so profound,
Turned them around,
Now red, now white,
Now black, now yellow skinned,
Green no longer.

So this is my tale for a pint of ale,
As you drink your glass of water.

THE DAY OF WRATH

Today is the Day of Atonement. What more can I say other than beware? How can I explain that which cannot be explained with logic? But this is my task since you ask so I will do my best to begin.

It is easy to judge your neighbour and to see his or her faults, but who can see their own shortcomings? In all honesty I can tell you that it is a monumental task on which few people would embark without a motive. It seems far easier to let things be, as change is hardly what one would want, unless one was unhappy with their present circumstances. And, if we are honest about the matter it would be clear that for most of the time we are happy.

It is easy to write pious remarks in prose and poetry, but to practice what one preaches, alas, is another matter! For example, if you say you'll do something, on reflection, you'll often find the willingness to do it is short lived or even non-existent. How often I've tried to improve myself only to discover a month or less later I am still the same after the euphoria of the initial effort has worn off.

So what can I say about a situation of which I am not fully aware? Who am I to espouse what I do not need? I can honestly avow that life is a process which we do not understand until it is too late. In reality there is no answer but who cares for reality when illusion is easy to come by? So the time is now as the message implies, where for a cigar or a cognac, happiness dies. Yet time is money and gold is honey, where bread is mouldy and broken.

The message is clear to all who hear, yet when will the cords be broken? The tune of tomorrow, with chords, resonant, strong and sublime for most of the time, but today all is chaos and discord. Yet who would believe it, yeah, who would receive it, without quiet desperation?

The answer is simple, like a computer program that makes the user lazy and lax like the measure of flax woven out of woe and wisdom. Who would object to the words of respect that the priest and the politician try to propagate? How can I say what I mean to say when I fear you will judge and condemn me?

The heart of the matter is that it cannot be denied that waffle makes for good reading!

SUBLIMINAL SEDUCTION REVISITED

Today there is no structure,
But it does not matter,
Or does it?

To live without focus,
Lacking direction,
Lacking a destination,
Is to live without purpose.

And yet,
To abdicate responsibility,
And to let others lead,
Is to play the victim,
To be a passenger,
Rather than the driver,
And it's up to me to choose.

Yet I am brainwashed,
Bombarded and bamboozled,
By sights, sounds, scents and sensations,
Subliminals and imbedded commands,
Pulverising my mind,
Taking away my power,
Manipulating, manufacturing and influencing,
So much so,
Do I know who I am?
And do I care?
Even I don't know!

RAMBLING ON MY MIND

In this field of inquiry what do I desire? A simple question as such that asks, oh, so much! Sometimes words are not enough, and the blind man calls your bluff without function or reason.

In this world I perceive it is impossible to believe in anything other than what I sense. It would be dense to deny what I hold in sight, in which I delight, other than for the sake of convenience. True, it would be easier, it seems, for calculated dreams are sometimes bright and rosy. But why would you care, if you were not there when I saw you. You were just in my head, though you've long since been dead and buried. Sometimes minds play tricks with definitions six times deeper than reality.

Oh, to perceive the truth you believe with my own perception. The world that I see, is it unique to me, or simply a mass hallucination? Am I asleep in a world of deep and meaningless inconclusions? And does it really matter?

JOURNEY

Alone in my head,
Alive, not dead,
I descend,
To the chamber of my heart,
Within my mortal frame,
Beating.

Beating and calling,
Calling to me,
Calling me to slow down,
Slow down and listen,
Listen to the silence,
The silence between the heartbeats,
Deep stillness,
Stillness and motion,
Balance and bliss,
Fluid, flowing and forever free,
Sanctuary,
Elusive and exclusive,
Where the butterfly has no master.

Alan Swift

SURRENDER OR DIE

Today is the day I die,
3pm June 27th 1543
Saturday afternoon,
They even hung my cat,
Today I will die,
Burning at the stake,
They call me a witch,
Those worshippers of a dead man,
A man upon a cross.

Mother Earth receive me,
Father Sky to thee I surrender,
Tonight I will run free with my ancestors,
For I cannot die.

Today I die and my baby within me,
For the Church wields its power with bloodshed and fear,
In the name of belief,
Blind and senseless are they,
Yet they kill,
Kill all who stand in their way.

Mother Earth receive me,
Father Sky to thee I surrender,
Tonight I will run free with my ancestors,
For I cannot die.

VERBAL MEANDERINGS

As he sat at his laptop his mind wandered down the alleyways of circumstance. Yesterday still imprinted itself upon his troubled mind. He wished he could remove it from his memory, but life was not that simple. He reflected on how it seemed that good things seldom lasted whilst bad things seemed to endure. Was it simply a human condition, or something more sinister? Christianity talks of a devil that plots against mankind. In the past he'd tried various systems of self-improvement only to end up where he'd started. Furthermore, he'd spent a great deal of time and money to no avail. He wondered if he would ever learn from his mistakes.

Observing his dreams and desires it occurred to him that they always changed and were never satisfied, even when they were fulfilled as he planned. This seemed strange to his reason; somehow logic could not fathom things out. The more he gained the more troubled he became and at one point he decided he would be happier without his material trappings, so long as he had health, companionship, a roof over his head and a full stomach. Yet he realised even that could not be guaranteed and eventually he would have to meet death. It seemed to him, without faith there are only losers in life and that all must fall into oblivion or worse. How could he know? It seemed so dire, so grim. Why were some people gifted or fortunate in life whilst others struggled with problems, which made his life look coddled?

He realised his questions had perplexed minds far greater than his for many years. He longed to believe in a loving God who loved and cared for him. Philosophies of formless bliss no longer appealed to him. He wanted happiness now and for all eternity without guilt or pain. The Bible now made sense to him in his suffering and sinful state. He realised he was just a victim of the devil's fury, but having accepted Jesus he was now delivered and saved. He had overcome for him and so life could not go wrong for he had been redeemed. At last life had meaning!

AMUSING MUSINGS OF MUSE

As I strolled in a field of lilies I was flummoxed to find the world God designed was, clearly, not perfect. How could it be, I just could not see as I reflected on the meaning of consciousness? As I thought hard and long I composed a song out of words and phrases, disjointed. Oh what could I do; so I drew a long view of my journey and the landscape before me? So there I stood and hewed the wood of epochs long and bitter. Though I thought it strange as words rearrange themselves before my eyes, like jugglers and ants of cosmic proportion. So I coolly collected myself, though from whence I came I know not and the sealed knot of seaweed and sand on the ocean so grand played before me.

Just then the clock of my mind struck one and reverberated in my brain like a juggernaut aflame consuming the grain upon the fret board of life. So there I stood like cosmic good and evil, stuck between them with little or no motivation. Time stood still aglow from the pill that had been taken from God by the randy little sod who claimed he needed it for pleasure and recreation. So then came a guy, oh way so high, proclaiming the truth was the answer. What does he know? Oh, I could show him a thing or three if he were but of the disposition to listen.

That was the last of him however grim the tale appears to be and you can but see that genius is next to madness. And the rambling rhyme is simply sublime without Bacardi and orange. 'Twas then that the maid said I hadn't paid my licence or public subscription. Caught by my host I consumed the toast that was on my plate and offered to wait for the bank to stay open. She flatly decreed that I must concede or risk a plate of fury and gall without a garnish of mercy. So there I stood a plank of wood held above my head proclaiming I was dead and defunct forever.

'Twas a familiar tale to those who sang in the vale just by the Welsh Borders. In fact the boarders were where they where because of circumstances naïve and make believe fabricated by their ancestors from long ago who did not know any better! As the night grew dim and the day grew weary Einstein had a theory of relativity that his mother-in-law would travel in time, oh sublime, to a tropical clime where budgies are roasted for breakfast, dinner and tea and compost is free provided you pay the waitress. So how do you know what you simply know when things seem new and impossible? It is like the eagle that appeared wearing a beard of infinite wisdom and beauty. Oh if only it would behave and simply shave then all the chicks would groove it! Dig this stuff man for if you understand it you're better than me at translating modern gobbledegook for a modern book of infinite trash and instant cash deposited into my bank account!

POCO IN ROMAN TIMES

Zeus sat in a seedy café with Frank and Diana drinking his fermented mead. Frank was a stocky character sporting a shaven head. His penetrating gaze revealed his enthusiasm for life, which was spontaneous and equally infectious. He sat there drinking his Grande latte displaying his love of learning in the words that he uttered.

Diana was of Mediterranean descent and her long black sensuous hair disguised her face, though revealing her feminine smile. She sipped on her goblet of milk as the scent of her spikenard filled the air.

Zeus had composed poetry before, but had had little published. Wanting to improve his skills he grasped with both wings this opportunity to meet with Frank and Diana as he had ambitions of becoming a famous author. He sat there munch on his wildebeest sandwich whilst simultaneously listening. Ever eager to develop, he would not be noticed by many, though tall and slender. Today is the birth of tomorrow he wrote and thus his career began.

POETRY OR PLEASURE

There was a lady,
So profound,
Her heart was restless,
And so was I,
But all that came of it,
Was this poem,
And an aching heart,
As usual.

And yet,
It matters not,
For I am content,
But will I always be?

What is life?
And what is death?
And who's the fool,
Who asks such questions?

THOUGHTS IN MY HEAD

Oh how can I claim to truly exclaim that which I don't understand? If a smile can launch a thousand ships, to where are they all sailing? If a heart can be bruised and broken by an infidel's kiss who is the traitor? If a picture can paint a thousand words what about Photoshop? Is it a new form of premature development that comes with too much exposure?

As the writer sat at his desk or upon his bed opening his mind he clearly designed words of cosmic drivel. Some people are inspired while others are tired and still others are tired of being tired of them. To separate the wheat from the chaff it is necessary to staff a panel of wise and learned judges. Alas, that costs money, and yea, that takes time, a costly venture indeed. So if these words you read seem beyond your comprehension bear with me a while as I compile a list of cosmic proportions.

The Bible by some is thought of as the sum of all God's revelation. Others would see the Bhagavad-Gita or the Dhammapada or even the Koran as more than the work of man, but only a fool would interpret a National Rail timetable. Yet that has been done, I tell you my son, though you probably would disbelieve me! The truth you see is practically free, just like the air that you're breathing. Yet man, poor soul, to earn a scroll, invented words of guilt and justification.

Let me laugh with you,
Let me cry with you,
Let me live with you,

Alan Swift

Let me die with you,
But first please tell me,
That you love me!

So now that you see, the artist is me, simply cough up the
due payment. As I need to eat and turn on the heat when
the weather gets cold and the budgies are sold to pay for my
parchment and pens. So what do you think of this waste of
ink and your precious, oh so precious, time? Well, whatever
you say as long as you pay, it to me, matters not!

I CAN SEE IT IN THE FUTURE

I can see it in the future, say a thousand years from now, that time travel will be developed. Travel backwards and forwards through all eternity will be possible. But if that is so, isn't it possible that it is here now? So perhaps modern day reports of UFO's and alien abductions may be visitors from the future!

The future is here now. The future does not exist and yet it does. Was Jesus a time traveller on a package holiday to Jerusalem many years ago? Did he lose his passport or did his time machine break down or get stolen? Is the future the past? Is it a cycle and will the universe run down only to start again?

Just then Gypsy Rose stood up and said "That's' all I can see in the crystal ball; your time is up and that will be ten pounds please!" I paid my fee and went outside her tent on a sultry June evening at the local circus fair and bought some pink candy floss.

TEACH ME TO LISTEN

Teach me to listen, Oh God,
To those nearest me,
My family, my friends, my co-workers.
Help me to be aware that,
No matter what words I hear,
The message is,
"Accept the person I am; listen to me!"

Teach me to listen, My Caring God,
To those far from me;
The whisper of the hopeless,
The plea of the forgotten,
And the cry of the anguished.

Teach me to listen, Oh God my Mother,
To myself.
Help me to be less afraid,
To trust the voice inside,
In depths beyond fathoming.

Teach me to listen, Holy Spirit,
For your voice,
In busyness and boredom,
In certainty and doubt,
In noise and in silence.

Teach me, Oh God to listen.

REFLECTIONS

The meaning of life is for all to see. At times we hurt and blame God for our problems seething with anger and resentment. She understands and stays quiet knowing that we will return to Her loving arms when the pain is gone.

Religion is a curse in many ways, especially when we cling to outworn creeds and dogma which we are afraid to shed even though we don't understand them. The truth is free but we prefer to buy other people's opinions rather than think for ourselves, especially as we get older.

The trust of man is hard to win once it has been frustrated. So often it seems the actions we perform are untold and unforgiving. Death can but stem the diet of me, but actions cannot be forgotten until tomorrow.

The remembrance of torpedoes and gusts of nuclear waste will fleet footed and swift in their haste, advance amidst the cries of hate and destruction. So who is the victor? And who the vanquished? Does not mankind understand that love, not war, is the answer? Is there an answer? Sometimes I wonder? Dear brother, dear sister, lay down your arms and can we but talk?

TWO FACED

I am afraid,
And that is why,
Why I wear a mask.

If I were to reveal,
Reveal the true me,
And you did not like me,
What would remain?
What would I have left?
Where could I run?
Where could I hide?

I would simply,
Shrivel up and die,
Or so I fear,
So that is why,
I wear a mask!

MORNING TIME COLOURS

Sometimes I wake in the morning,
Desolate, despondent and down,
Wanting to die,
But that is just because it's morning.

As I come to,
As the day goes on,
My mood improves,
But not always,
But then I remember,
That life is a game,
And most blessed am I,
Blessed with many talents and gifts,
And I have so much to be grateful for.
I can see my lover in the morning sun,
I can taste the sweet wine of joy upon her lips,
I can kiss and caress her scented body,
I can hear her sensuous lilting voice croon,
"Alan, I love you and want to be with you always!"
And isn't it grand to walk hand in hand,
Through the dew soaked grass,
In the morning!

So if you are down,
And feel life is without hope,
Hang on in there my friend,
For one more hour,
For one more day,
For life can only get better,
Of that you can be certain,
And death is not the answer!

SPACE

Space and time, in infinity sublime, keep from sight, the dust of spite. For what is perceived will follow on, outside of eternity. So keep your thoughts to yourself if you want good health. Have a smile, one for you and one for me, and then you'll forget you're blue like the sky above and fall in love. Think mere mortal; ponder!

Quit the pit and flee the sea, which rages and rattles whilst the rain falls on the ground with a ceaseless rhythm, pitter-patter. What is this load of fish and rambling garbage composed in the head, better left unsaid, better unread by all but the twelve beyond the cosmos where reason is no longer needed?

One day in June upon the moon a silver spoon of cosmic dust bit the crust and filled with lust as was just and proper, and saw the verge begin to purge the city of grime and crime whilst as if in a dream of vast proportions. It was claimed by those who knew that the world was like a dewdrop in the lotus footprint in the sands of time, as the gods and goddesses did sport and play for yesterday does not exist outside of the mind of its creator.

FOR ALL THE TIMES I FORGOT

Dear Dad, for all the times I forgot to say "Thank You" I'm
sorry.
There's so much you've done for me and so often,
And yet I've just accepted it without a word of thanks or
praise,
I've done it so often it's become a habit,
So this is just to say,
Thank you Dad, for all you've done,
And I love you.

For the times I've never appreciated you I'm sorry,
For the times I've accepted your help without a word I'm
sorry,
For the times I've refused to put myself out I'm sorry,
For the times I've misjudged you, misunderstood you,
And put myself first,
I'm sorry Dad.

Thanks for your care for me,
When I was a child and you had to work,
Thanks for taking good care of Mum and me,
Thanks for putting us first,
Thanks for all the sacrifices you willingly made,
Thanks for your love and protection,
Thanks for your prayers and correction,
Thanks for taking me to church,
Thanks for having me baptised and confirmed,
Thanks for being there for my first communion,
And thanks for never giving up on me,
For letting me be,
For this and much more, thank you Dad.

Sometimes I take things for granted,
Sometimes I say silent,
Yet there is often a time to speak out,
And although nobody's perfect,
And it's all too easy to criticise,
For the times I've hurt you I'm sorry,
I love and appreciate you,
More than words can say,
And I know Jesus loves you too;
Sometimes the road is long and winding,
And the way seems dark,
Yet Yahweh knows the way and has a plan for all,
Surely Jesus must have wondered when on that cross,
Or why would he have said,
"My God, My God, Why have You forsaken Me?"

The darkest hour is before the dawn,
His greatest gift to us is being born,
So do not despair,
And remember,
Jehovah loves you far more than I possibly can.

I'll just close by saying thanks for being you,
And thanks for having me,
And thanks for being there when you were needed,
Shalom Aleichem,
God bless dear Dad,
Amen.

(Originally written and read to my Dad on 27th April 2003 as an exercise in gratitude and an expression of love. I've edited this slightly so it scans better. My Dad passed away on 2nd December 2011)

POWER THINKING WITH BROTHER MANDUS

The year was 1945 and I had just escaped from the prison of the storehouse of my mind. I found myself seated on warm white sand in a secluded bay. The sun shone brightly overhead, challenging scurrying pastel shaded cotton wool clouds to dim its rays. Seabirds wheeled overhead calling merrily to each other, telling of their escapades and adventures. Either side of me rose majestic cliffs of basalt and granite, dappled green and grey in the afternoon sunlight, interspersed by crimson flowers adding to the glory of this natural scene.

Directly ahead of me rose a dome shaped rock of similar structure, being roughly twenty to thirty feet in height. Seated upon this rock was Brother Mandus (Of the World Healing Crusade in Blackpool England) who had come to teach me as I slept on my bed on Monday 9th June 2003 at 2.45am, I knew it was him, though I could not make out his features. In fact I didn't really see him as such, but I instinctively knew it was him. His voice, commanding and authoritative was familiar, yet kindly. It was as if I were talking to an old friend, as indeed I was. I saw many things and heard lofty words backed up by experiences beyond description. At last I was free to advance beyond this mortal realm to the stars of heaven and further.

I clearly heard his voice enquire "Why wait until you are eighty or ninety years old to get healed my friend? Why be unhappy, waiting until you die? Why wait for God to take you from this world in which He has placed you? God wants you to be happy now, my son, my daughter, my child! May these words bring you and others comfort and compassion. As the Father has loved me, so do I love you! I can heal your thoughts if you will but let me!"

Brother Mandus' words echoed in my mind, healing and rejuvenating my soul, gladdening my heart at this unearthly hour just before the summer sun rose in the year 2003 so far from the seashore which lingered sufficiently in my mind for me to remember upon my awakening; and thus I put pen to paper and began to write: The year was 1945 and I had just escaped from the prison of the storehouse of my mind.

BATTLEFIELD OF THE MIND

Warrior of the Lord,
Prepare your mind,
O valiant disciple of Jesus,
Awake,
Slumber is not for you.

Ace of spades, four of clubs,
Divination rubs you up the wrong way,
Forget your dreams,
Forget your desires,
There's a battle for your soul my child.
Deception and deceit are the weapons,
Forged with offers of fornication for the feeble,
Draped in power, piety, prestige and self-restraint for the
more mature,
The battle rages on beside the doorstep of desires,
And alone you cannot win,
So trust in the blood of the Lamb,
Victim and Victor!

Disciple of the Holy Spirit,
Prepare to serve Jehovah,
Choose your master well,
Leave your pride behind,
The deceiver will try anything,
When you resist him.
Only the weak will survive,
Trust in the Lord and lean not unto thine own understanding,
The Prince of this world controls all religions,
Though that is better forgotten.

Words of power,
This is the hour,
The time has come,
Get off your bum,
Proclaim Jesus, Lord and Saviour,
And embrace the Beloved One.

Only yesterday I died,
Yet nobody cried,
Or so I thought,
Forgetting the price,
With which I was bought,
For Yahweh doesn't take things lightly.

Agarashi oni mani upitini asini olati opaniaum oftinei
Jesu ofltile ompani oftenti alimani ogarashi,

Jesus is the Victor,
Words of power,
This is the hour,
The time has come,
Get off your bum,
And proclaim Jesus Lord and Saviour.

LIFE WITHOUT REASON

Death cannot redeem you,
Life cannot forgive you,
You may look the other way,
But that will not change things.

Nature is relentless,
Nature just is,
It does not judge,
It is like gravity,
You cannot argue,
You simply have to understand,
And then and then alone,
Can you reclaim your authority,
For wisdom is power,
And power is knowledge,
But love conquers all.

Life cannot condemn you,
Death cannot imprison you,
You can always look the other way,
But what then?
The situation still remains.

IT'S A BEAUTIFUL DAY FOR DREAMING

"How much must I pay, dear Lord?"
Said the miser to the Master,
Searching for salvation,
Unaware of the birds and flowers,
That blossomed all around him.

How much must I pay for each breath that I take?
Each step that I make?
Each morning I wake?
Each word that Thou spake?
In this world of untold goodness.

Fools seek salvation in Heaven,
Whilst life on Earth passes them by,
Yet there is no tomorrow without today,
So while the sun shines on you,
And the wind ruffles your hair,
Smile,
For in your heart,
You know you are worthy!

Surely, as they must,
Bad days may come,
And good days may go,
For this is a land of impermanence,
But don't get down or wear a frown,
For things will turn out okay,
If you just, but let them!

I NEED TO TALK TO MYSELF

If perchance I read this rambling rhyme,
And find it gives me comfort,
I must apply it to me and me alone,
And not to my neighbour.

When I see my sister's failing,
Manifesting so clearly,
I need to stop,
I need to look within.
When I see my brother's brazenness,
I need to stop,
I need to look within.

What I see on the outside,
Is but a reflection,
In the mirror of my mind,
But f by chance,
The mirror is distorted,
What will I find?

What in my neighbour I see,
Is but a part of me,
So this poem is for me,
And me alone,
For I am all that's here,
And when my spirit,
This body leaves,
This life,
No longer will matter,
Even though this world will probably continue,
Though there is no way I can prove it!

Yesterday is but a memory,
And tomorrow is but a dream,
And words of blissful ecstasy,
Are but a scheme,
Born out of wilful manipulation,
By a skilful scribe,
Trying to earn his daily crust,
So I will not despair,
Or pull out my hair,
When I finally bite the dust.

So if perchance you read this rambling rhyme,
And find it gives you comfort,
That's okay,
But I originally wrote it to remember,
That I am just a man,
And I don't want to be perfect;
Do you?

BLOOD ON YOUR PLATE

I'm sorry,
Blood has to be spilt,
I'm hungry!

And yet,
To look at you,
Young, beautiful,
Long blonde hair,
With innocent eyes,
And a beguiling smile,
I would not think of you,
As a killer of animals.
And yet,
Here before you,
There on your plate,
Lies the now cooked carcase or chop,
Of an animal that once was so cute,
That you got someone else,
To butcher,
To kill,
To slaughter it for you.

Generation on generation,
Has feasted on bacon and eggs,
Blindly not knowing of the suffering,
And I too was guilty and I too must pay,
But I cannot turn away any longer,
So please,
If you must still eat meat,
At least cut down,
For the sake of your conscience.

PURPOSE

Never turn another down,
And never turn away,
Never withhold your tender touch,
From a cry for help and love,
Never turn down a chance to care,
For a bleeding heart,
Dying from despair,
Just because you feel unsafe,
Never leave your blessings,
Until it's far too late.

Greet the dawn as it is breaking,
And welcome the sun as it rises,
Bringing forth another day,
And always be glad.

Never turn away,
In fear or in anger,
For life is too short,
To entertain misery and woe,
And laughter is a universal remedy,
And it is your destiny to love and to serve,
In happiness and joy.
So begin today to smile,
And gain the satisfaction,
That you've helped another,
No matter who,
And never,
Ever turn another away.

WHY DO POETS BLEED

As I roved out one morning early,
I met a maid fair and comely,
With flowing locks of jet black hair,
And a smile so alluring,
Her eyes were like jewels,
Set in alabaster,
Her lips like pomegranates,
Ripe for the harvest,
Her cheeks rosy and full,
Her frame sensuous and provocative
And yet now I only have memories,
Memories of her carefree laughter,
As my heart she ripped asunder,
Memories of tears,
As she left,
In the night,
So long and dark,
Memories of her embraces,
Torment my languishing soul,
And yet how could I be so naïve,
And will I ever learn,
And is Mecca really a bingo hall,
Just next to Safeway?

ILLUSIONS

Is it possible to sweeten your daily dreaming?
Is it possible to lighten your nocturnal visions?
Is it possible to find peace and calm this instant?
It is possible if you are willing to try!

The method is easy and simple,
It is this:
You must stop!

Stop running from the past,
Stop running from the present,
Stop running to the future.

The method is easy and simple,
It is this:
You must give up denial!

Give up denying what your heart knows is true,
Give up denying what lies behind and ahead,
Give up denying this present moment,
And give up illusion and fantasy,
For in truth you are responsible,
For your life,
And your reality.

SONG OF SILENCE

Suffering soul,
Can I make you whole?
Where is your beginning,
Your middle and your end?
Is there an end?
And yet does it really matter?
Spirit souls languishing in the dark of the night,
Eternity evading our grasp,
As we sink beneath the waves of consciousness,
Drowning without hope,
And yet we still are,
And always will be.

WITHIN

Buried deep inside,
Lie tears of bitter anger,
Attended by hatred,
Unwilling to acknowledge,
The pain, the guilt and the rage within,
Resentment transubstantiates itself,
Leaving a fear of silence and idleness,
And a bitter aftertaste,
Called depression.

WORDS ARE BUT WORDS

I heard them say that you had a good innings,
That it was for the best that you go,
Yet ninety years or more,
Is but a day with little more to show,
With life left behind you now,
And your former joys and your former sorrows,
No longer matter.

When you finally awaken,
You'll no longer cry,
For now you live,
And can no longer die,
Though those on Earth,
May grieve for you,
Yet time will heal,
Even their hearts,
And their memories will blur,
For that is the way,
Whilst living there.

So today they will cry their tears for you,
For now they miss you,
And perhaps always will,
Until they reach the golden land,
Beyond yonder hill,
To see the sunrise breaking,
On eternity's horizon,
As a new day dawns,
Beyond this land where life means death,
For all that are born.

ALAYANA YAKATANA!

Alayana Yakatana!
You say you do not believe,
In life after death!
So tell me,
Dear doubter or wisdom,
Do you believe,
In night after day?
Tomorrow after today?
Sunshine after showers?
A world of love and flowers?
Or have you abandoned all hope?

Alayana Yakatana!
Does the Earth slumber,
When the evening sun sets,
To dream of eternity without sorrow?
Does the Moon console her seven sisters,
Smiling in the night sky,
With tears running down her cheeks,
An infant at her breast
Eager to be born,
In a world where love is the law?
For thus it is my friend,
If you think so!

Alayana Yakatana!
Why do you think this way?
Is it not better to be happy in Hell,
Than sad in Heaven?
So don't grieve for what cannot be,
And simply do the best you can.

FINALE

Say you're working on the final chapter of your life and you're waiting for it to end. You may be tired and frustrated but full of questions and may wonder what the next chapter will be, and maybe, will there be a sequel. It is like going to sleep at night. It is natural and you always wake up to greet a new day; don't fight it.

And if you follow my advice literally and get burnt you only have yourself to blame. You chose to listen to me and not yourself, so you believed and you acted and you reaped what you'd sown.

And if you question your occupation thinking "Is this a life?" and the answer you receive is "Yeah!" then that's okay and stick with it no matter what others may say or do. Be true to yourself and, yeah, stick with it.

I write because I can. There is no other reason. I breathe because I can and it's in my nature (and my doctor recommended I keep it up!).

I write because I write. Like the mountain and the valley. They just are. And it is so. There are no other reasons nor need there be any (though fame and cash are nice!).

The wise do not question nor do they listen. And I am a fool for the learned aren't wise or foolish and neither is so.